Cincinnati Art Museum

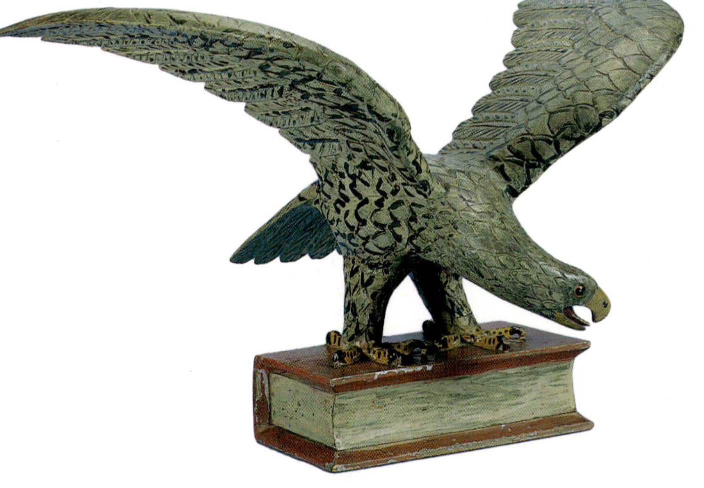

The Fine Art of Folk Art

by

Anita J. Ellis
Curator of Decorative Arts

Genetta Gardner, Ph.D.
Associate Curator of Painting

Dennis Kiel
Associate Curator of Prints, Drawings and Photographs

Otto Charles Thieme
Curator of Costume and Textiles

The Fine Art of Folk Art
Exhibition dates:
May 11 - September 2, 1990

Photography by Jeff Bates
Typesetting by Craftsman Type
Printed by Dai Nippon
Designed by Noel Martin

ISBN 0-931537-12-6

The Cincinnati Art Museum gratefully acknowledges operational support from the Cincinnati Fine Arts Fund and the Ohio Arts Council.

Cover illustration:
Yosemite Valley, L. A. Roberts,
See page 18.

Introduction

Anita J. Ellis, Curator of Decorative Arts
Cincinnati Art Museum

The purpose of this publication is to offer a sense of the depth and quality of folk art collections in Ohio. We often, if not always, look to the East or the Southwest for America's great folk art collections. Indeed, those areas can boast a proud history of collecting. One need only note the exceptionally fine collections of the Abby Aldrich Rockefeller Folk Art Center in Colonial Williamsburg, Virginia, the Shelburne Museum in Shelburne, Vermont, and the Museum of International Folk Art in Santa Fe, New Mexico, to see that this is true. What seems to have gone unnoticed is the rich collecting of folk art in the Midwest, especially Ohio. Until now, the Akron Art Museum has been the only museum to recognize this in published form with *American Folk Art In Ohio Collections*, 1976. Collecting in Ohio has been active since at least the 1930s, if not earlier. Not only collectors, but many folk artists themselves have been at work in Ohio. Such artists as Elijah Pierce and Nan Phelps are nationally known, while others such as Robert McWilliams and Edward M. Hageman are known only locally, but probably not for long. Although a publication of this size cannot fully credit the scope and quality of folk art collecting in Ohio, it strives to contribute towards that end.

Joining me in this project are three colleagues from the Cincinnati Art Museum: Dr. Genetta Gardner, associate curator of painting, Dennis Kiel, associate curator of prints, drawings and photographs, and Otto Charles Thieme, curator of costume and textiles.

The following entries need little explanation except to say that all measurements are expressed in inches, in order of height, width and depth. The initials at the end of each entry are those of the curator who selected the piece and wrote the entry. Folk art in its broadest, most generic sense was used as the basis of selection. This is one publication that makes no attempt to question or strictly define folk art. Only pieces produced in the United States and Canada were selected to allow for a more manageable focus.

Many people deserve recognition for this publication. First of all, I wish to thank the Ohio Folk Art Association, the collectors and artists who generously offered their objects for scrutiny and publication. They are the *sine qua non* of the project. Assistant Director for Development L. James Edgy, Jr., Assistant Director for Operations George E. Snyder, Jr., Designer Noel Martin, and Editor and Manager of Publication Productions Carol Schoellkopf deserve special acknowledgment for deftly putting the project together and seeing that it reached the printed, published form. Sincere gratitude also must go to photographer Jeff Bates, registrar Ellie Vuilleumier and the staff of the Registration Department at the Cincinnati Art Museum who made the illustrations possible. Definitely not forgotten are those who assisted in the curatorial departments: Cecie Chewning, associate curator of decorative arts; Lynn Bilotta, assistant curator, art of Africa and the Americas; and Sarah Johnson, clerk typist, Painting Department. I salute my colleagues Dr. Genetta Gardner, Dennis Kiel and Otto Charles Thieme, who joined me in the belief that folk art in Ohio collections deserves recognition. And, I commend Director Millard F. Rogers, Jr. for his vision and support throughout.

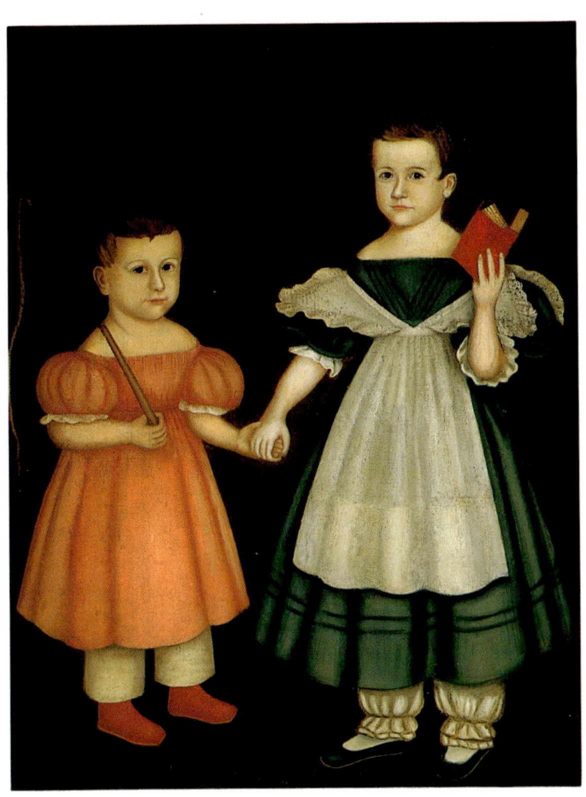

Children of a Judge from Painesville, Ohio

1820, Unknown Artist, Ohio, 51 x 39 inches, oil on canvas, Collection of Alice and Richard Guggenheim.

According to an inscription attached to the back of this painting, these are the "Children of a Judge from Painesville, Ohio, Painted by an Ohio Artist, 1820." Although verification has not yet been discovered, the inscription provides a fascinating explanation of who these charming children are. The artist who painted them had considerable talent in modeling the forms and applying color. In typical folk fashion, he posed the two children frontally and depicted them with their favorite objects. The boy (left) holds a whip, and his sister (right), a red book. They congenially join hands, by adult insistence, we suspect. GG

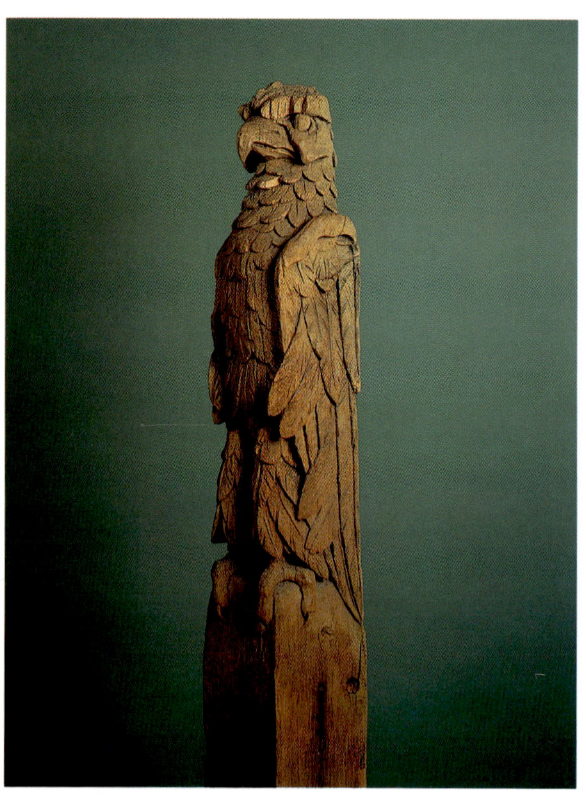

Eagle Fence Post

Last half of the 19th century, Unknown Artist, Ellerton, Ohio, entire post 65½ x 5 x 5 inches, eagle 25 x 5 x 5 inches, carved wood, Collection of the Cincinnati Art Museum, Anonymous Gift, 1986.907.

The Eagle Fence Post was donated to the Cincinnati Art Museum by a collector who discovered it partially hidden under a mound of hay dust and seed on a farm in Ellerton, Ohio, near Dayton. Dowel holes cut into the sides of the post below the eagle, and mortises on the rear of the post indicate it was originally part of a fence. The eagle gives no evidence of ever having been painted.

The carving is particularly intricate. The feathers are individually treated and the talons of the bird are so deeply undercut that the eagle appears to be resting *on* the post rather than simply being an extension of it. Indeed, the form of the entire bird is restricted to the five-inch depth and five-inch width of the post, and yet it gives no sense of being bound by those dimensions. It is a majestic depiction of the Nation's emblem, the bald eagle. It is rare that the eagle displays such power when its wings are folded. AJE

Appliquéd Quilt

1850-70, Unknown Artist, United States, 99 x 91½ inches, red, green and white cotton fabric, appliquéd and quilted, Private Collection.

This quilt encapsulates all the joy the artist must have had in creating a vigorously designed colorful object. The energy of the four traditional large red and green "Princess Feather" motifs rotating in place is barely contained by the bordering vines. Although the feathers and fronds appear to have been cut from the same template, the rhythms of their quirky placement move the viewer's eye in fits and spurts throughout the composition. Even the axis of central floral design is given a rakish twist.

With a singleness of mind and exquisite eye, the artist maintained her design concept throughout the weeks necessary to appliqué each piece in place. The simple diagonal line quilting must have served only to hasten the move of the quilt from the frame to the bed. OCT

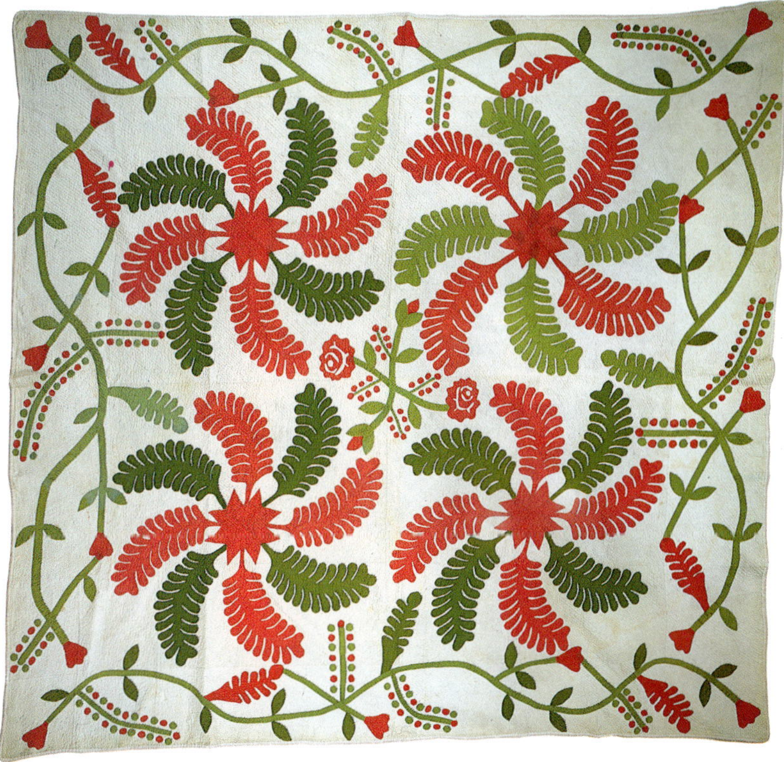

Fractur – Certificate of Marriage and Birth for Asa K and Sally Blake

Ca. 1817, Unknown Artist, Pennsylvania (?),
13¼ x 11½ inches, watercolor with pen and ink on paper,
Private Collection.

Fractur script, a writing style derived from medieval manuscripts, came to America with the Pennsylvania Germans. With the addition of a variety of decorative forms, "fractur" became a general term for all art indigenous to the community. It was most commonly associated with birth and baptismal certificates.

This fractur by an unknown artist is unique for its celebration of a marriage and birth in one document. The perfectly symmetrical design is framed by a small floral border with "hex" signs at each corner. The angel stands at the center of the "tree of life" and, as indicated by verse 7 of Psalm 122, bestows "peace" and "prosperity" upon the family.

The inscription appears to be incomplete. The tightly balanced composition is disrupted somewhat by the irregular spacing within the three hearts. Based on the existing design, a second row of type (with her husband's name?) was probably intended to accompany "ASA K." The comma following "BORN" is also an indication that, like the "MARRID" heart in the center, a third line with the date was meant to be included. DK

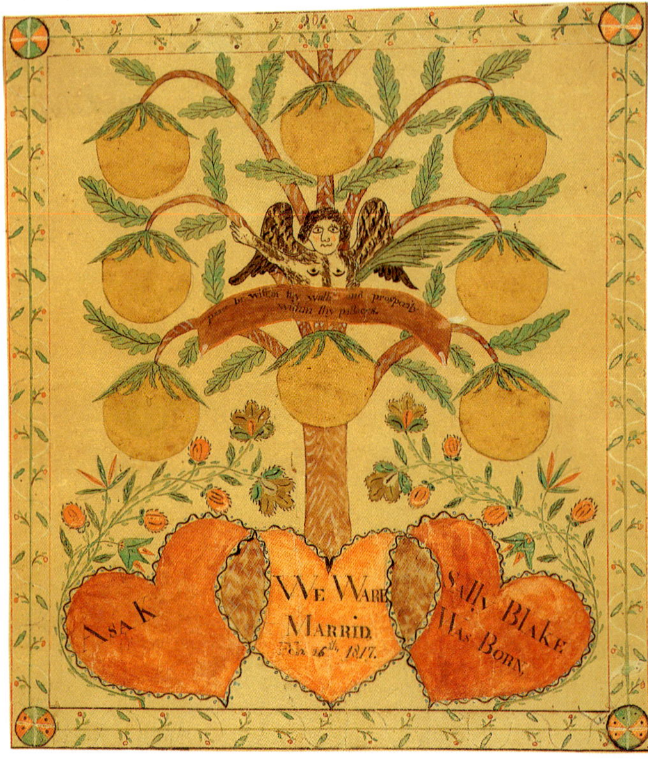

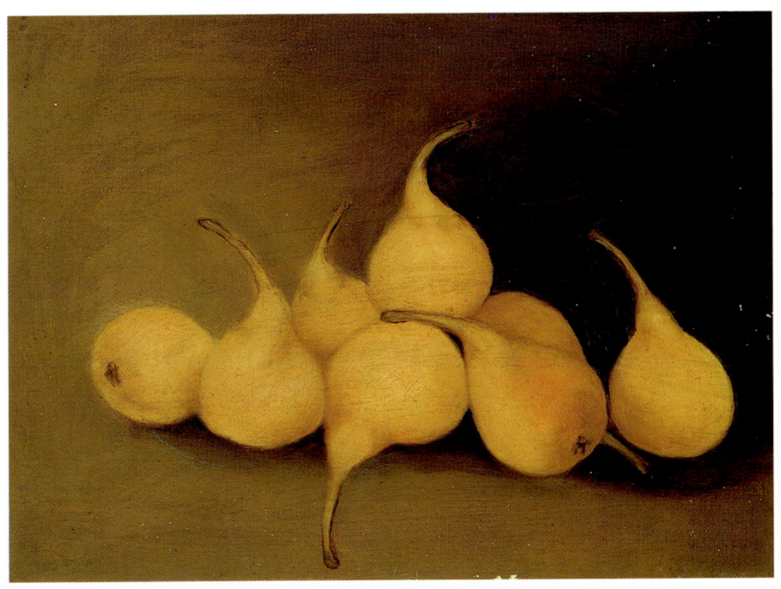

Pears

Early 20th century, Rhoda Steddom, Warren County, Ohio,
8½ x 11½ inches, oil on canvas, Private Collection.

These luscious fruits have the warmth of tonality and sensuous drawing of a still life by Chardin. The artist, however, is Rhoda Steddom, from the Turtle Creek area of Warren County, Ohio. All that is known about her life is that she married her grade school and high school teacher, Marcus Mote, a Quaker. Judging from the age of the canvas, she must have lived in the late nineteenth and early twentieth century.

Still life painting has had a rich tradition for centuries in Europe and the United States. During the seventeenth century, paintings of abundant fruit often symbolically represented the ephemeral quality of life, while covertly signaling the wealth and prosperity of the patron. For Rhoda Steddom, the pears, which she so carefully rendered, may have been a recording of a bountiful fall harvest. Yet the intimacy of the little picture and its subtle coloration goes far beyond documentation, to suggest the pleasures of taste. GG

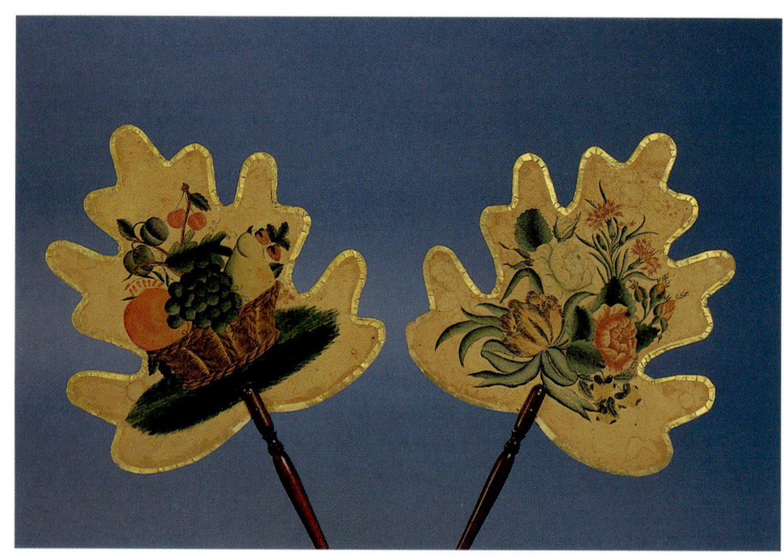

Two Hand Screens

Ca. mid-19th century, Unknown Artist, each approximately 16⅝ x 9⅞ inches, watercolor and gilded paper on cardboard attached to wood handle, Collection of Dr. James and Susan Widder.

The fireplace was a focal point in every early American home from the mid-seventeenth to the mid-nineteenth centuries. It functioned as the primary source for both heat and light. Hand screens (also called fire screens or candle shades) were often used to protect the face and head from the flames of the fire. They were made from a variety of materials ranging from exquisitely embroidered silk to the more popular and more affordable engraving on paper.

Based on the folding fan, these two hand screens, unusual for their leaf-like contours, were painted on rigid cardboard, elegantly trimmed with gilded paper and attached to handles of turned wood. Although the fruit and flower arrangements have a similarity to watercolor theorems (stencil paintings) and were probably derived from these schoolgirl patterns, both compositions appear to have been executed without the use of stencils.

On the reverse sides, flowers, fruit and birds surround examples of the artist's penmanship: two didactic poems devoted to beauty and friendship.

When not in use, the more decorative hand screens were frequently displayed on the mantelpiece. By the 1900s, this arrangement became an important design element for most American fireplaces. DK

Untitled – The Bee Fight

Ca. 1910-20, George Frenk, Dayton, Ohio,
20½ x 26¾ inches, pastel on canvas, signed, lower right edge,
''George Frenk,'' Private Collection.

Not much is known about George Frenk, the artist of this pastel, except that he was active in Dayton, Ohio, during the early part of this century.

Country life was a popular theme among artists at this time and Frenk has recorded an amusing moment among friends and family. Six boys, many with paddles in hand, and two dogs are fighting what looks like a losing battle with a swarm of honey bees. Although the boys could be robbing the bees of their honey, their actions, especially the boy poking at the tree stump with a pole, appear to be frivolous at best.

Drawn with broad areas of color and sweeping diagonal lines, the young boys are strewn across the canvas in a variety of stilted poses. Combined with the contrasting stipple effect of the leaves, the course of action is almost as difficult to follow as the flight of the bees themselves.

The ominous size of the insects may be Frenk's warning that what seems like a playful activity does have its drawbacks. Bees do sting, and the child seated at the far right appears to be tending to a wound. The boy in the center has a bee on his head and the little black dog is definitely in for a very big surprise. DK

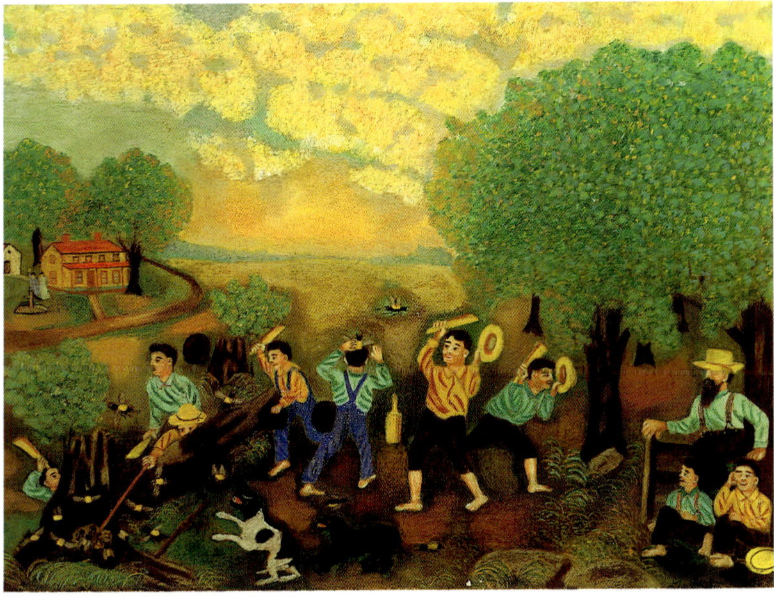

William Penn's Treaty with the Indians

Ca. 1835, Edward Hicks, 1780-1849, Pennsylvania, 22¼ x 28⅛ (with frame), oil on panel, Collection of Mrs. William T. Earls.

Among primitive painters of the nineteenth century, the pride of place goes to Edward Hicks. Born in Attleborough (now Langhorne), Pennsylvania, in 1780, Hicks was raised by a Quaker family after the death of his mother. As a young man he apprenticed in carriage making and later in 1801 established his own business in partnership with Joshua Canby. His thoughts, though, were fixed on spiritual matters, and in 1803 he joined the Society of Friends, becoming a forceful preacher. Business losses caused Hicks to turn from carriage making to carriage painting, and through this he discovered his true talent for painting. By the age of forty, he began creating oil paintings drawn from engravings of paintings by other artists.

One of his best-known works is *William Penn's Treaty with the Indians*. This subject was first painted by Benjamin West around 1692; it was later engraved by John Hall in 1775 and published by John Boydell. Hicks used the engraving of West's painting and woodcuts in Watson's *Annals*, 1829, of Penn's landing at Chester and in Philadelphia, to fashion his own version. The painting proclaims to the Indians and the world the Quakers' desire for a peaceable society. GG

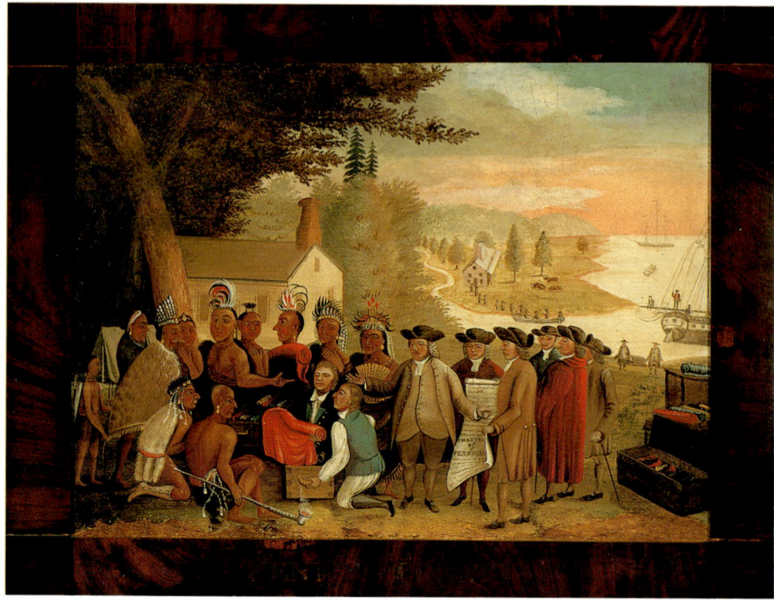

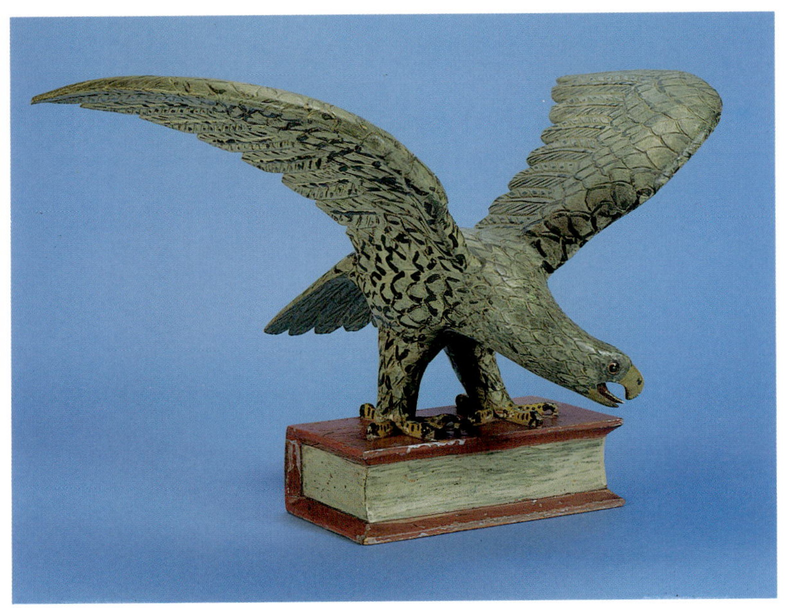

Eagle on a Book

1820s-30s, Unknown Artist, Pennsylvania (poss.),
16¼ x 24¼ x 18½ inches, carved and painted wood,
Private Collection.

The bald eagle became the American national emblem in 1782 and has since become the most commonly used animal in American folk art. Eagles with aggressive stances are particularly symbolic of the United States.

This noble specimen, perched heroically on a book, is of a type found in Pennsylvania. A similar example can be seen at Old Sturbridge Village, Sturbridge, Massachusetts. There the eagle is described as standing on a Bible. The book here has no lettering and its title cannot be determined. Perhaps the identity was lost with a new layer of paint that was added in the distant past. In any event, the Bible would have been a logical complement to the eagle since America was such a God-fearing nation. This example and the one at Sturbridge are so similar that they could be by the same hand. The Eagle on a Book is exceptional in its design and execution. AJE

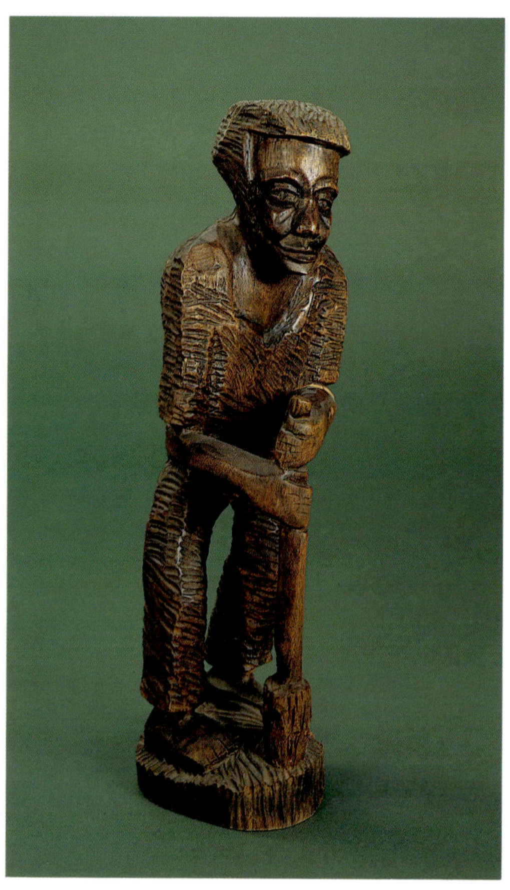

African-American Worker

1930s (poss.), Unknown Artist, Midwest or the South, 18 x 4¾ x 6 inches, carved wood, Private Collection.

The African-American Worker was purchased during the summer of 1987 in East Port, Michigan. With it was another carved African-American portrait signed "J. Noel/1937." Whether the two are by the same artist is unknown. Circumstantial evidence of wear and association with the other dated piece suggest a possible execution date during the 1930s.

Also unknown is the ethnic heritage of the sculptor. Whatever the artist's background, the work is a sympathetic depiction of labor. The figure is at a moment of rest as he leans on his tool. The tool is identical to the wooden pestles used by African-Americans in the South to winnow chaff from the rice grain. The pounding mortar-and-pestle method of winnowing was used on southern rice plantations from the 1690s to as late as 1940. The worker could have been carved from life, from memory, or from oral tradition. AJE

Pink Pig

Ca. 1970s, Nellie Mae Rowe, 1900-1982, Vinings, Georgia, 16 x 20 inches, crayon and felt-tipped pen on paper, signed, lower right, "Nellie Mae Rowe," Collection of Lois and Richard Rosenthal.

Nellie Mae Rowe was raised in a family of ten children in rural Georgia, just outside of Atlanta. As a child she loved to draw and spent many hours creating wildly imaginative images based on her own dreams. Rowe produced very little art during her adult life, but began drawing and painting incessantly after the death of her second husband in the late 1940s. Making up for lost time, she became somewhat of an eccentric by covering her entire house and yard with her own artistic creations, personally handmade dolls, nicknacks and assorted found objects.

Unlike her early line drawings, *Pink Pig* has an expressive quality, with its bold colors and complex arrangement of fantastic shapes and animal forms. Any explanation behind what appears to be an expectant pig with her foot on a wheel inside of a heart shaped form is unknown. The decorative nature of the tree at the lower left, however, may very well be a reflection of her African-American heritage.

Nellie Mae Rowe remained a practicing artist until her death in 1982. DK

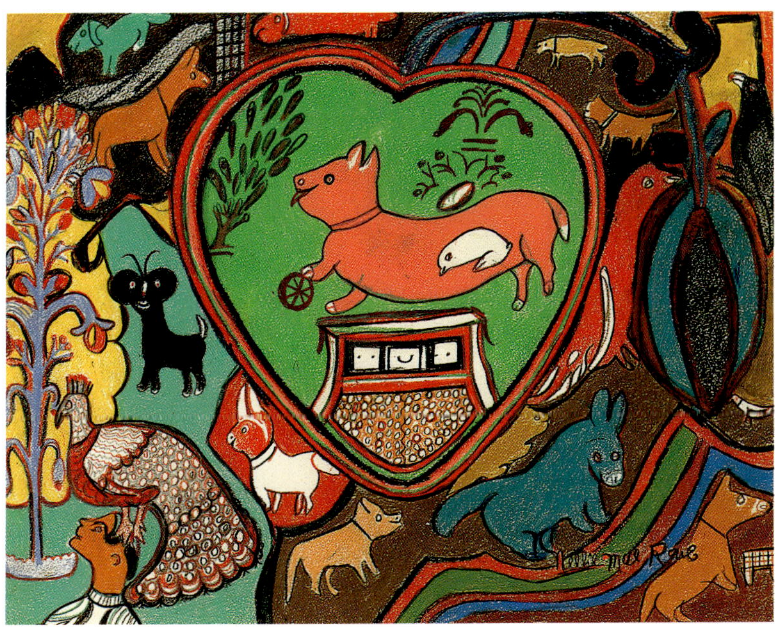

Boy with a Hoop

1830s, John Bradley, active 1831-47, New York City, 40 x 30 inches, oil on canvas, Private Collection.

John Bradley or I. Bradley, as he signed his name using the archaic form of I for J, is listed in the New York City directories of the 1830s and 1840s as a portrait and miniature painter. He signed over twenty paintings but little else has been discovered about him, with the exception of one painting signed "I. Bradley from Great Britton."

This painting is documented from the Southwich family of New York. The boy is formally presented in an interior with a hoop and a large fur hat that is turned upright on the star-patterned rug. The view through the window shows the boy's reward for patiently posing for his portrait. In this delightful scene he happily rolls his hoop down the street, wearing his great fur hat. GG

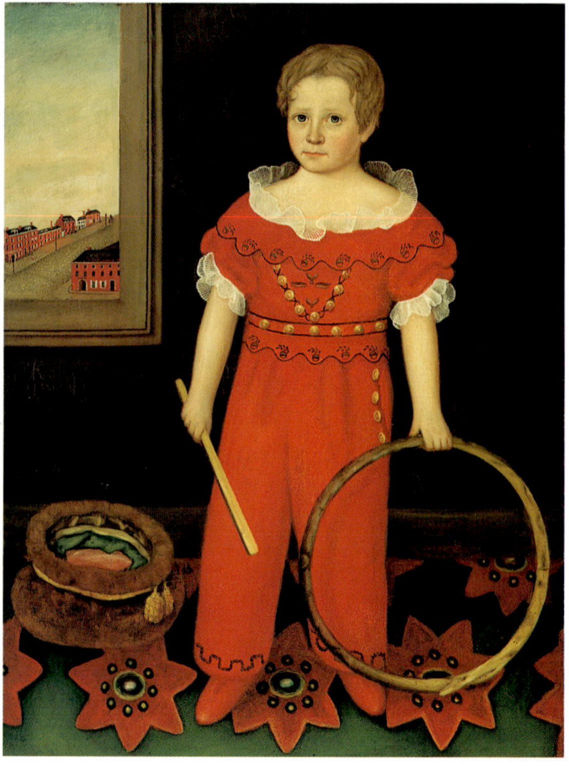

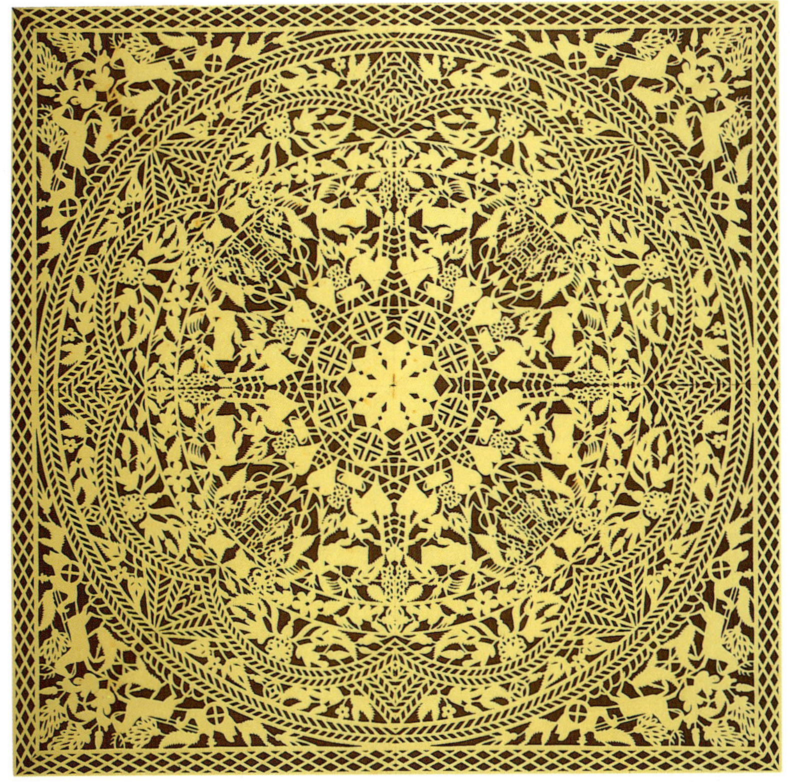

Cutwork Valentine (?)

Ca. 1890s (?), Unknown Artist, Pennsylvania (?),
39¼ x 39¼ inches, cut paper, Collection of Shari Knight.

The art of cut paper or "scherenschnitte" (scissor-cut) originated in the Far East and was brought to America by the Germans. Combining their own tradition of border cutouts with silhouette portraits, this unique craft was very popular among fractur artists, especially in Pennsylvania, during the early nineteenth century.

Most "scherenschnitte" pictures were generally folded in half or into quarters. The design was then added in pencil and precisely cut with scissors or a sharp blade. They were used primarily to decorate birth and baptismal records, valentines and, on rare occasions, mourning pictures.

This elaborate cutout is the result of six intricate folds. The artist has carefully constructed an array of patterns that mirror each other unexpectedly throughout the design. Details include a stag and carriage, and a cross, heart and angel with crown and anchor, a possible reference to faith, hope and charity. Complex and incredibly large in scale, the work is an example of technical virtuosity at its finest. DK

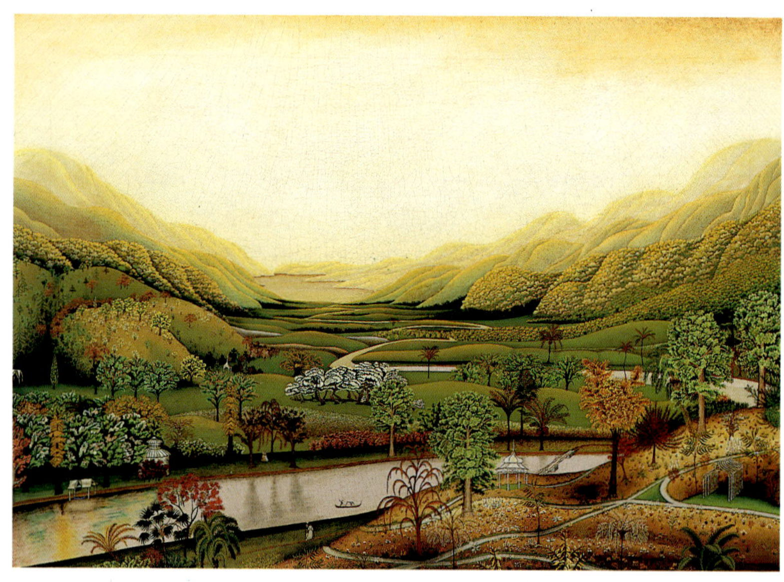

Valley Landscape

Early 20th century, L.A. Roberts, 33 x 46 inches, oil on canvas, signed, lower right, "L.A. Roberts," Collection of Cincinnati Art Museum, Gift of Mary M. Clift, M.D., 1967.316.

L.A. Roberts is a painter of unknown origin. Nevertheless, two paintings by him appeared in the Over-the-Rhine area of Cincinnati in the early 1930s. The landscapes belonged to Dr. James Alfred Clift, who acquired them from an elderly couple living near Findlay Market.

For years the identity of the artist was unknown, but during a recent cleaning of *Valley Landscape* a signature in the lower right corner was discovered. Attempts to uncover additional information about L.A. Roberts or to locate other works by him have so far been unsuccessful.

Although the life of L.A. Roberts remains a mystery, his paintings reveal a wonderful idiosyncratic sense of landscape. *Yosemite Valley* must have been painted from a photograph, but *Valley Landscape* is pure imagination. Exotica, such as coconut palms, a gondola, and gazebos, decorate a rolling river valley enjoyed by strolling visitors. Botanical inventions flourish; their rich color harmonies form a fantasy of paradise. GG

Yosemite Valley

Early 20th century, L.A. Roberts, 33¼ x 46¼ inches, oil on canvas, Collection of Cincinnati Art Museum, Gift of Mary M. Clift, M.D., 1967.317. (Illustrated on front cover)

Cane

1863, Unknown Artist, probably southern United States, 30 x 2 x 2 inches, carved, incised, and painted hardwood, Collection of Mr. and Mrs. Roy Waits.

Only an inspired carver could have looked at a length of hardwood and visualized this combination of form and image. A man's head forms the knob handle; his stand-up collar marks the passage from the handle to the cane itself. Below the knob, a dog's head turns into a spiraling snake form, whose tail grasps the lower portion of the cane.

The artist placed his most intricate forms in this lower section. Around the straight shaft of the cane, a green and black snake entwines itself. Bright red beads are placed in the snake's eyes. Perched between its sinuous curves are a black monkey, two green and gold lizards, a black donkey's head and numerous small gold-painted knobs. All these figures are undercut and raised off the surface of the shaft. Sheet brass encases the tip.

Elaborately carved canes of similar form and imagery have been documented as products of an African-American wood carving tradition. Although the original significance of the cane has not been preserved, its dramatic presence continues to command our attention. OCT

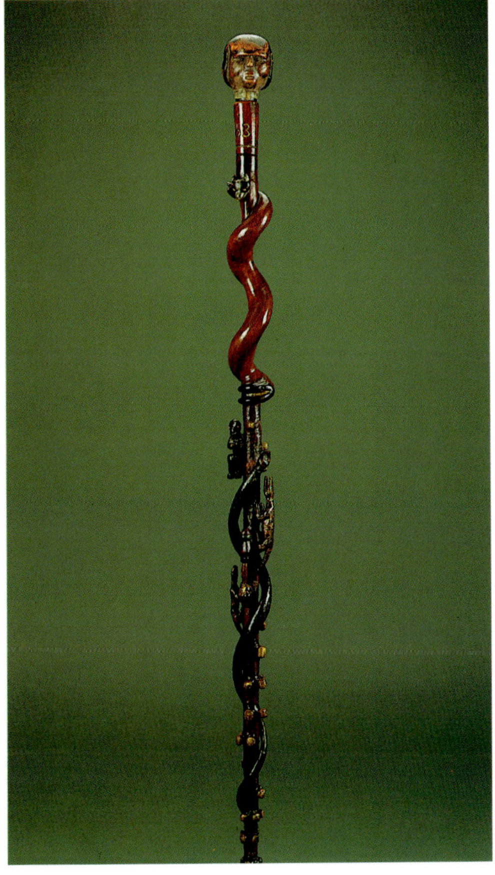

Rooster Weathervane

Ca. 1850, Unknown Artist, Levis, Quebec,
with stem 30¼ x 14 x 3⅝ inches, formed and painted tin,
Collection of Dr. James and Susan Widder.

This weathervane was originally over a Christian roadside shrine in Levis, Quebec. In Quebec the rooster is referred to in the native French as a *chanteclêr.* Rooster weathervanes are also called weathercocks. It is not unusual to see the bird atop shrines and churches in Canada as well as in the United States. Besides announcing the call to matins with its crowing at daybreak, the rooster, or cock, is featured in the New Testament as it crowed twice following Peter's three-time denial of Christ.

The Rooster Weathervane is all hand formed and was probably made by a tinsmith or whitesmith, as the tinsmith is often called. The body of the bird is hollow. The parts were originally cut from sheets of tin, probably from a pattern, then bowed, or pressed around a wooden form to give the shape, and finally joined together. The wings and especially the tail feathers are simple design patterns that give the rooster its sense of identity and presence. In all, it is a very simple almost abstract form generating the impression of command and dignity. AJE

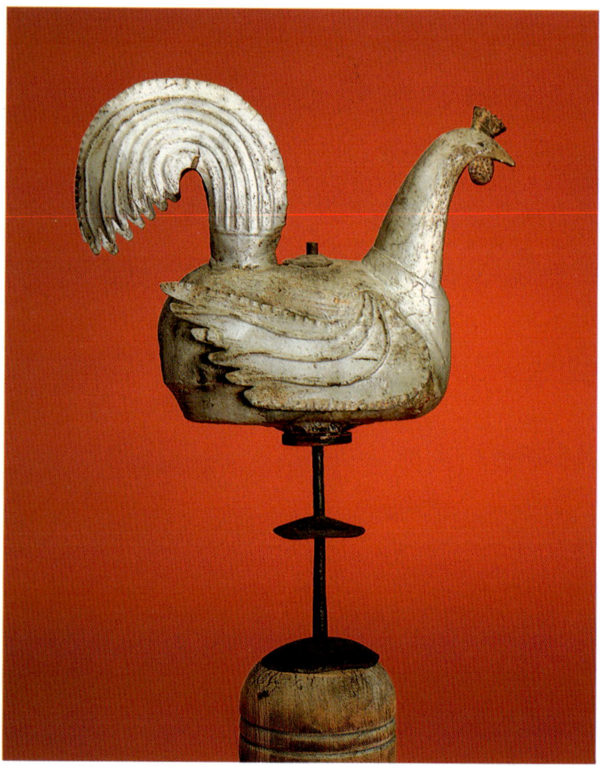

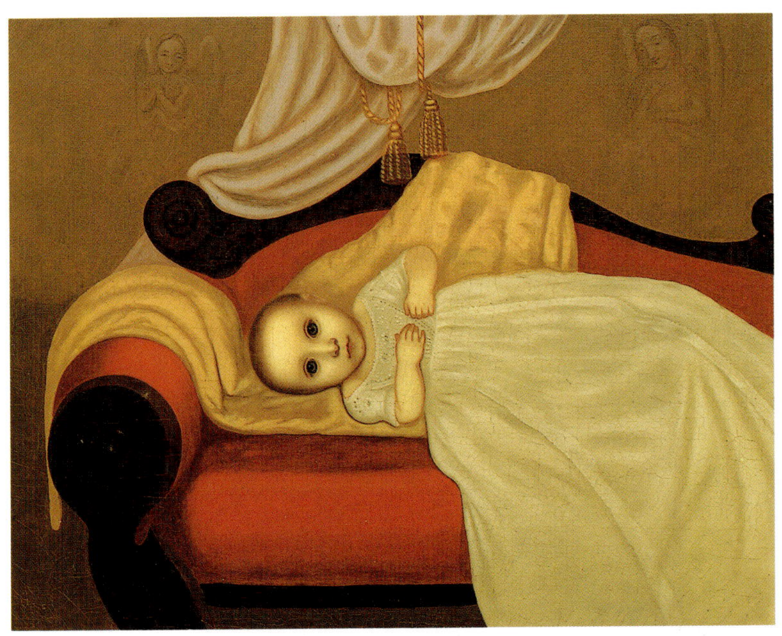

Infant

Late 19th century, Unknown Artist, 22 x 27 inches, oil on canvas, Collection of Alice and Richard Guggenheim.

In folk portraiture children are frequently portrayed standing, frontally posed, holding a toy or flower, and occasionally accompanied by an affable pet. Infants are usually represented in this same manner, but sometimes they are portrayed in their mother's arms, awake or sleeping, or propped against a slightly older sibling. This painting, however, is atypical of any known types of infant portraiture in that it shows a baby reclining alone on a red empire sofa. The infant is further distinguished by its remarkably blue eyes that stare directly at the viewer. Moreover, in the upper corners of the painting are two thinly painted angels.

The presence of wraith-like angels and the shroud-like drape on the sofa suggest that the infant may be dead and that the painting was done as a memorial to a lost child. However, the alert expression of the baby indicates otherwise, showing that the picture served as an invocation, in the tradition of Renaissance painting where adoring angels protectively watch over the infant Christ Child. GG

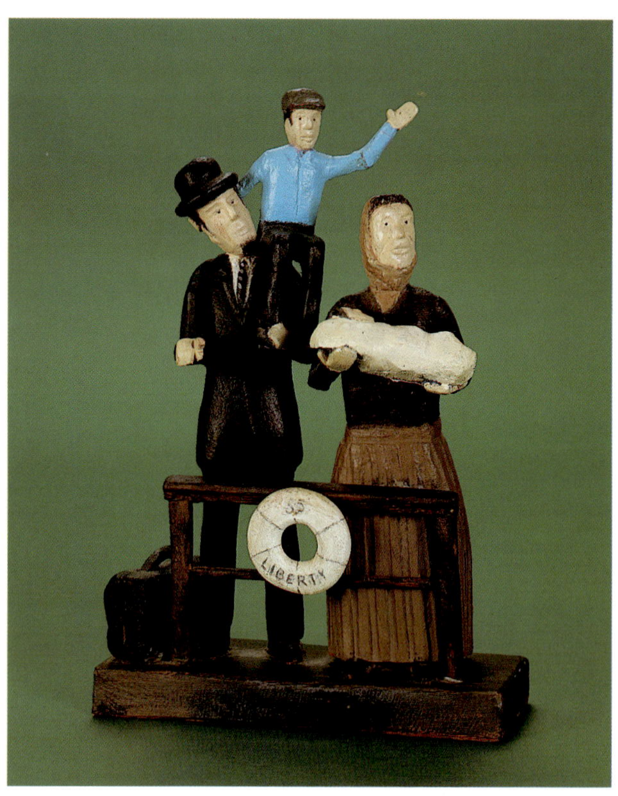

U.S.S. Liberty

Ca. 1977, Sol Landau, b. 1919, New York City, 15 x $9\frac{3}{4}$ x 4 inches, carved and painted pine wood, inscribed in black on bottom "Sol Landau," Collection of Lois and Richard Rosenthal.

Sol Landau is a contemporary folk artist living in New York who is noted for anecdotal subject matter relating to family life. He might depict a boy being fitted for his first suit with father watching proudly and mother crying at this right of passage, or a Jewish father showing his child a mezuzah.

Here Landau depicts an immigrant family sailing into New York. The notation on the life preserver tells all: U.S.S. Liberty. The quartet is arriving in the land of freedom and opportunity. It is a life experience common to the family history of so many Americans. The expressions of hope are real, and it is not difficult to assume that their eyes are fixed on the Statue of Liberty.

It is interesting to note that the definition of this scene rests almost entirely on the life preserver and its lettering. The preserver tells us that this family is on a boat; and "U.S.S. Liberty" tells us the family is coming to America. Without this prop the scene would lose its meaning. AJE

Getting from One Day to the Next

1982, Robert McWilliams, b. 1939, Oxford, Ohio,
24½ x 25 x 19½ inches, carved and painted wood, and wire,
Collection of Robert McWilliams.

Robert McWilliams began carving in 1972 at the age of 32. His original inspiration came from a great-uncle who whittled. This inspiration along with a collection of old tools led him to woodcarving. McWilliams has a Ph.D. in geology and is an associate professor at Miami University in Oxford, Ohio.

His carvings are based on wit and insight. In this example, "Getting from One" is on the horizontal band at the bottom; "Day to the Next" is on the reverse. We see people precariously going from the sun to the moon, struggling to get from one day to the next. It is a comment on the frustrations of everyday life. Getting through another day is all that one can ask. AJE

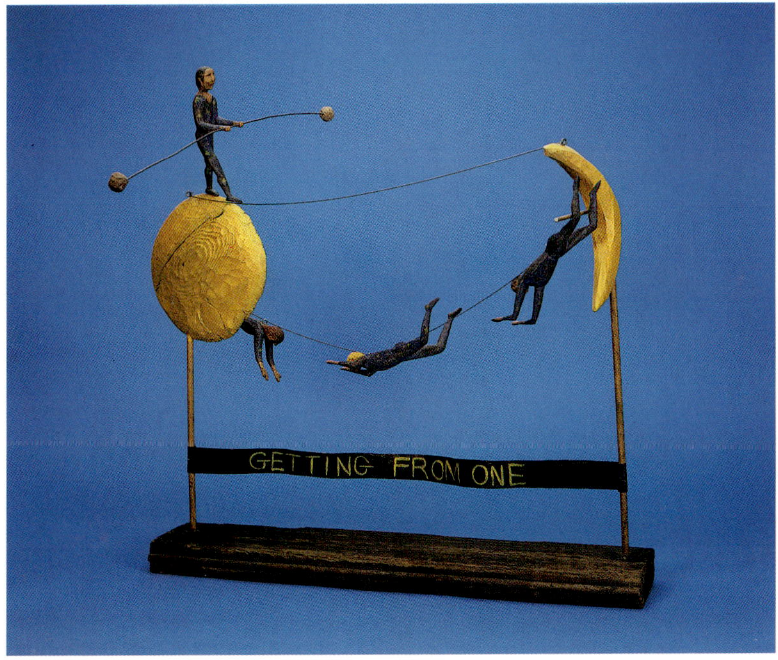

Waterfall and Two Fishermen

1850, Unknown Artist, 34½ x 27⅛ inches, oil on canvas, dated on back of canvas, "1850," Private Collection.

Contrary to the colorful landscapes typical of folk art styles, this fascinating painting was executed in monochrome, limited to a palette of only black and white. As a result, the landscape takes on a wintery chill, appropriate weather for the fleece-lined coats worn by the fishermen. In a delightful contradiction to the foreground scene, three sailboats drift across the distant lake, suggesting an artist's flight of fancy in hopes of more moderate weather.

Landscape painting such as this, which emphasizes the monumentality of nature in comparison to man's more modest size, was a popular theme in nineteenth-century American painting. The cut-down tree in the foreground served not only as a compositional element, but was also a popular symbol of the progress in the settlement of the western United States. GG

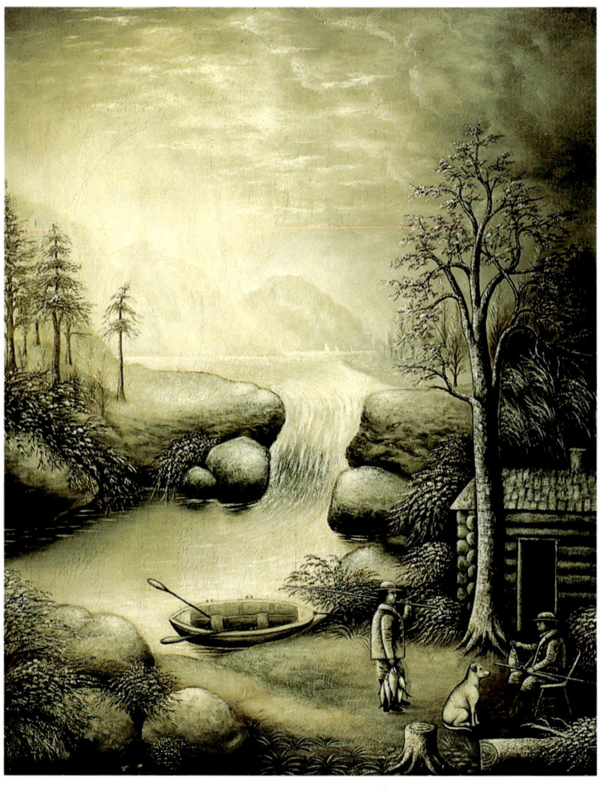

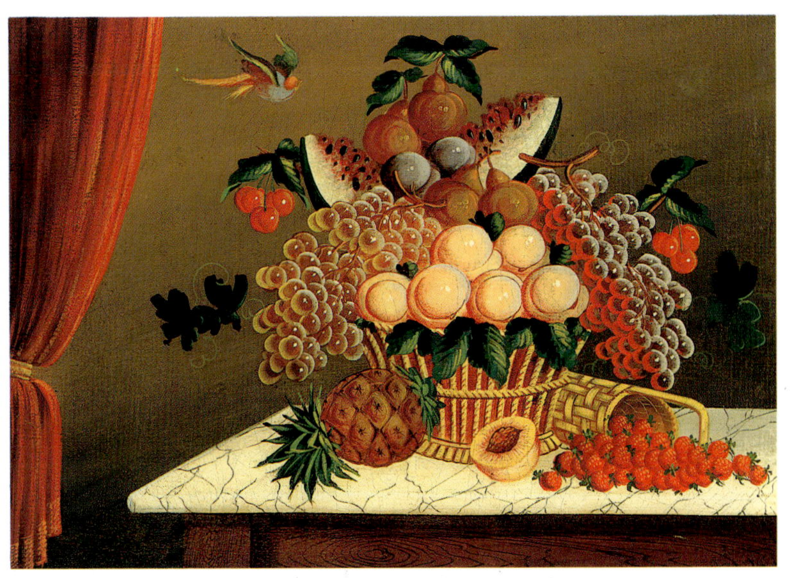

Still Life with Fruit and Bird

Ca. 1850, Unknown Artist, 29½ x 21 inches, oil on canvas, Private Collection.

Like seventeenth-century still life painting, this work contains an arrangement of fruit, demonstrably luxurious and grouped without regard for accuracy of the growing season. Peaches, cherries, pears, grapes, and watermelon are collected in a wicker basket. Spilling from a smaller basket onto the marble top table are strawberries. A pineapple is at the left. The purpose of this painting was to present an ostentatious display of rare and delicious fruit; its exotic nature is enhanced by the colorful bird which is about to discover a sumptuous meal. Still within the tradition of Baroque painting, a curtain is painted at the left, drawn and tied back, to reveal the marvelous display. The artist has taken obvious delight in bright colors and pride in a bountiful harvest. GG

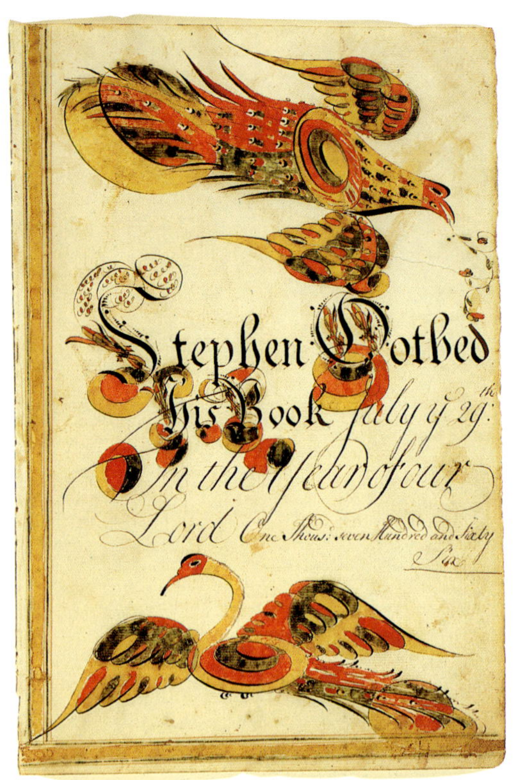

Title Page from a Book of Weights and Measures

1766, Stephen Gothed, $12\frac{1}{2}$ x 8 inches,
watercolor and pen and ink on paper, signed, center,
"Stephen Gothed," Private Collection.

Good penmanship was a sign of culture and status during the eighteenth and nineteenth centuries. Writing schools were established in most major cities and itinerant instructors offered lessons in the art of calligraphy throughout much of rural America.

In this example, Stephen Gothed's superior penmanship is apparent in the bold gothic styling of his name and in the use of two cursive variations for the date and year. The exotic calligraphic birds, drawn as a decorative extension of the stylized script, are composed of looping pen lines of varying thickness. The experimental use of color adds both opulence and vitality to the written page.

Gothed may have been a writing master. This page, therefore, would probably be an example of the demonstration pieces or writing samples (also called writing slips) that instructors often produced to promote their work. On the other hand, it might also be a student's academic exercise, serving the dual purpose of teaching penmanship as well as information about weights and measures. DK

Crow

1979, Edward M. Hageman, b. 1910, Dayton, Ohio, 8¾ x 14½ x 4 5/16 inches, carved and painted wood, incised on bottom, "Edward M./Hageman '79," Private Collection.

Edward M. Hageman began carving in 1977 at the age of 67. The winter of '77 was particularly bad, and during a blizzard with nothing else to do, the artist took a knife and went to his basement for an old piece of wood and began carving. His choice of subject matter can be humorous, such as a fish with its mouth open to show a human arm holding a fishing pole, or a delightful reflection on nature, such as this crow.

The artist carved the bird from photographs of a crow that frequented a dock in Florida where his daughter was living. While the bird is simple and elegant in form, it not only gives the essence of the species, but it also suggests an individual personality. AJE

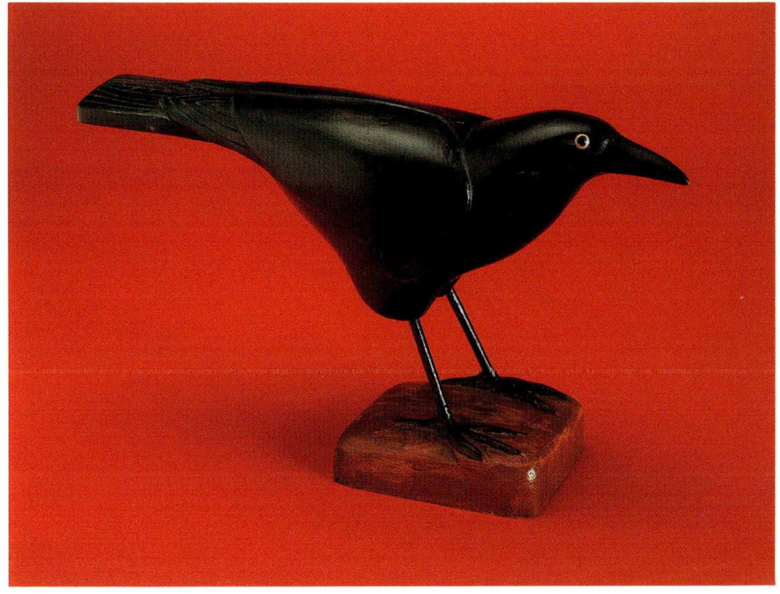

Indian Archer Weathervane

Last half of the 19th century, Unknown Artist, Tucson, Ohio,
21½ x 17½ x ½ inches, cut and painted sheet iron,
Collection of Mr. and Mrs. William Gilmore.

This Indian Archer Weathervane stood over the Improved Order of Red Men's lodge in Tucson, Ohio, six miles east of Chillicothe. The Improved Order of Red Men was a national benevolent fraternal organization. The archer represents Saint Tammany, the symbol of the order. Saint Tammany was a Delaware Indian chief esteemed by the colonists. It is not known when the weathervane was removed from the lodge. In the twentieth century the weathervane was acquired by Wallace and Pearl Gray. The Grays owned the general store in Tucson. Mr. Gray also owned a blacksmith shop and was a Red Man. While he owned the weathervane it was used during Red Men powwows at Tara Hollow, near Chillicothe. One "Indian" stood on a corner and used the weathervane to point the way to the Tara Hollow powwows. While the Indian archer is a common subject in weathervanes, this one is peculiar because of the pine tree depicted behind the Indian. It is perhaps a symbol unique to the Tucson, Ohio, Red Men. AJE

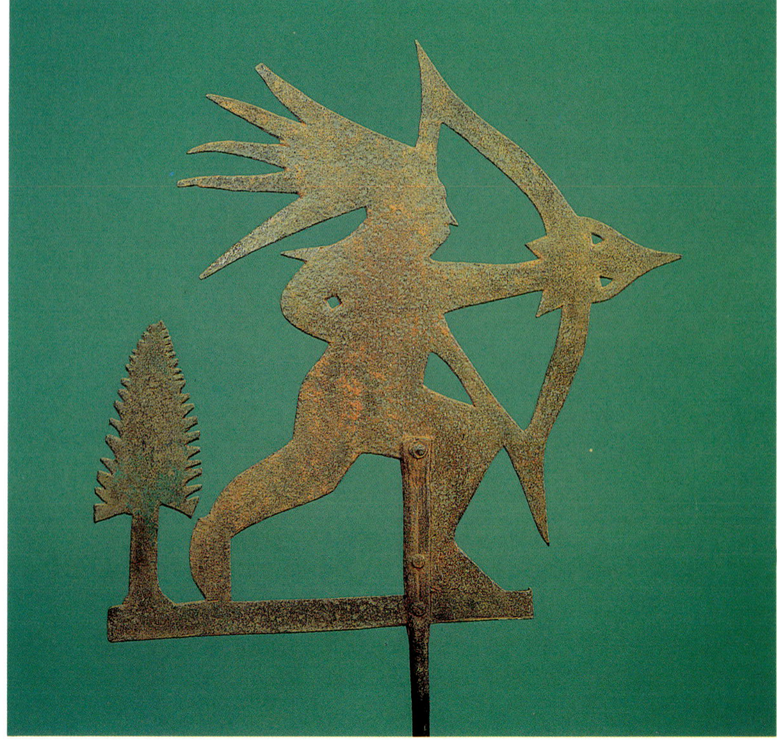

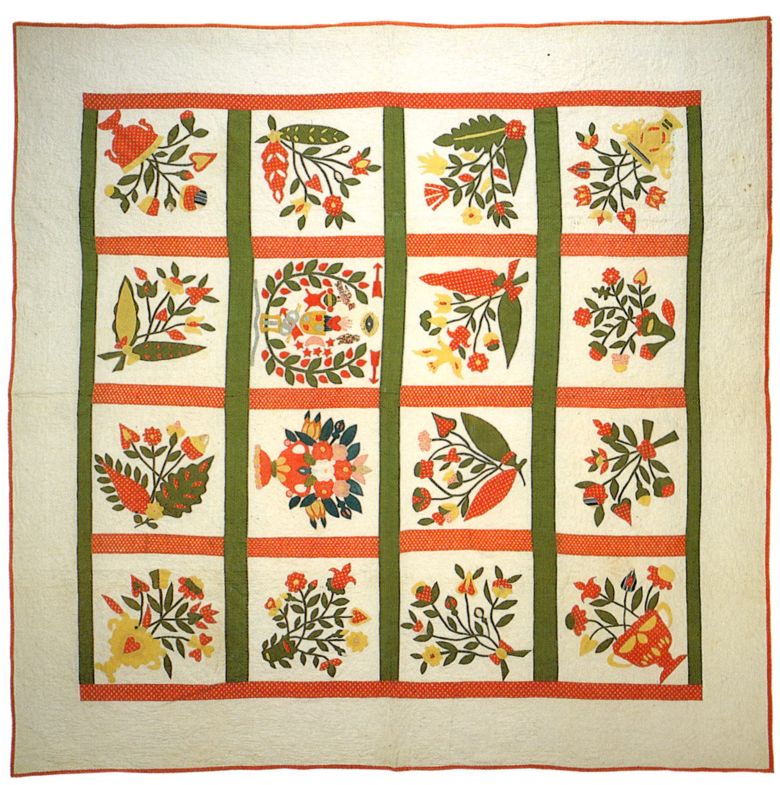

Pieced and Appliquéd Quilt

1840-55, Unknown Artist, United States, 97 x 96½ inches, various dyed and printed cotton fabrics, appliquéd, pieced and quilted, Private Collection.

The album quilt format is useful for assembling disparate elements into a unified whole. Of the sixteen appliquéd squares on this quilt, fifteen are variations of two compositions – a vase of flowers, and a bouquet of flowers. However, no two squares are alike. The sixteenth and most complex square is comprised of Odd Fellow symbols placed inside a red and green wreath. Although a few textile patterns dominate, a total of twenty-one different, dyed and printed cotton fabrics are used for the appliqué. Some, such as those used in the "eye" on the Odd Fellows square, appear only once. The use of long unpieced red and green strips to frame the album squares suggests that the quilter combined both small scraps and much longer lengths of cloth.

While joyful invention seems to mark the composition of each square, order is imposed by the quilting. Diagonal lines are quilted only in the red and green grid, stitched floral motifs appear only within each of the sixteen appliquéd squares, and an undulating leafy vine circumnavigates the whole in the outer border. OCT

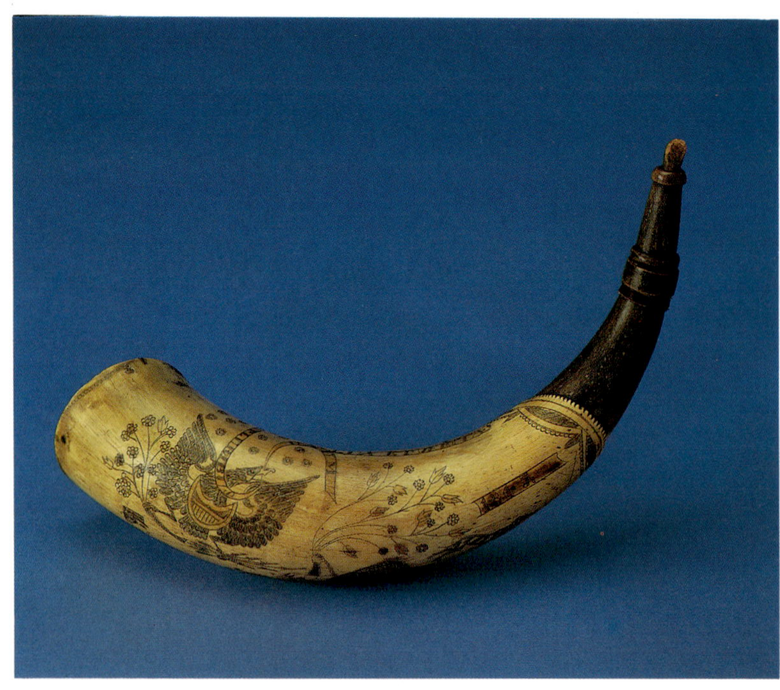

Powder Horn

1845, Unknown Artist, Indiana, 11½ inches, carved and incised horn, wood, Collection of John Diehl.

In many ways the leather shirt, the hand-bored fire-arm, and the powder horn symbolized the frontier male ethos. Even rudimentary skill could transform the horn of a bull or ox into this object of great necessity. The smooth surface was easily scratched, and many men used incising to decorate their powder horns.

Great care was lavished on the decoration of this powder horn which was used as a presentation gift. The dedication is inscribed on one side: "Present from John McCutcheon of Indianapolis to David C. Ringland of Newburg, Lux et Veritas, James K. Polk, 1846." The end of the horn has been carved away to form the rounded tip from which the powder was poured, and below the tip, the grooved ring served to anchor a leather carrying strap. A serrated edge divides the tip from the base.

The base of the horn is as exuberantly decorated as the top is plain. Elements from three vignettes spread out to eventually cover the surface of the horn on all sides. In one vignette, a horseman puts a trumpet to his lips and charges after a dog who is in pursuit of a doe. In another, a young woman – adorned with a flower-bedecked bonnet, lace mitts, and a low-necked short-sleeved dress – carries a flowing floral bouquet. Her skirt is short enough to display her pantaloons. The largest vignette features an eagle derived from the image on the Great Seal of the United States. Beneath an array of fifteen stars, the eagle clasps in its beak a flowing banderole inscribed: "E pluribus unum." OCT

Portrait of a Girl with a Lemon

Mid-19th century, Unknown Artist, 40 x 25½ inches, oil on canvas, Collection of Mr. and Mrs. Tom Porter.

The diminutive size of children permitted their depiction in full length and allowed them to be surrounded by domestic details. Here the little girl, in a white eyelet decorated dress, holds a lemon in her left hand and flowers in her right. Close beside her is a favorite kitten. The interior is well appointed, indicating the little girl's parents' prosperity. It is decorated with stenciled carpet, chair, and table with a vase of flowers. The artist has added a paned window with a view of a river. The artist also painted pendant portraits of the parents, belonging to the same collection. As in the portrait of the daughter, the parents are placed in their home, a setting that best displayed their prosperity. GG

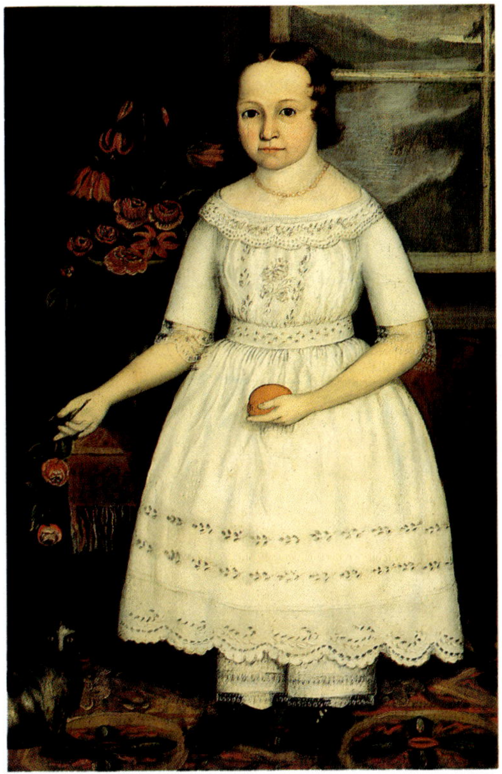

Pieced Quilt

1800-50, Unknown Artist, United States, 80 x 65¼ inches, various wool fabrics pierced and quilted, Private Collection.

At first glance this quilt appears to be a hodgepodge of color, pattern, and placement. The artist seems to answer to no formalized visual code, no pattern tradition. Perhaps.

This is not a display quilt. It is not made from new cloth specially purchased for the project. There is no meticulous measuring nor painstaking stitching. Over twenty different kinds of heavy wool cloth were saved from other uses, selected and arranged by the artist, and simply quilted. She not only formed a large warm covering, but also produced a visually rich object. Working within the constraints of materials at hand, the artist consistently placed the same blue fabric in the center of each of the pattern squares. Most of the shapes appear to be roughly measured, then sewn to fit.

Thè artist created a superb composition of the best modernist sort, as color and its sophisticated placement form a composition alive with surface movement and a sense of depth. If the art in folk art is the creation of a personal aesthetic statement while working within a traditional format to create an object for everyday use, then this quilt is a masterpiece. OCT

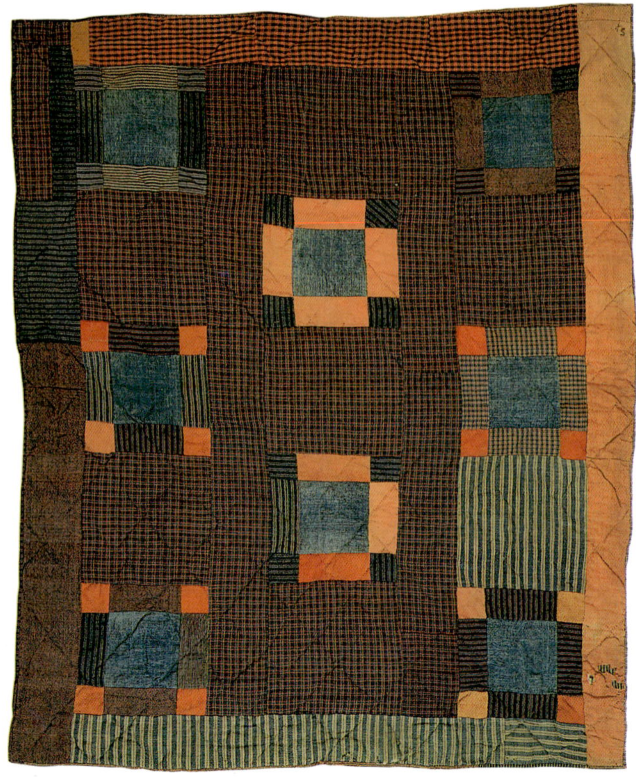

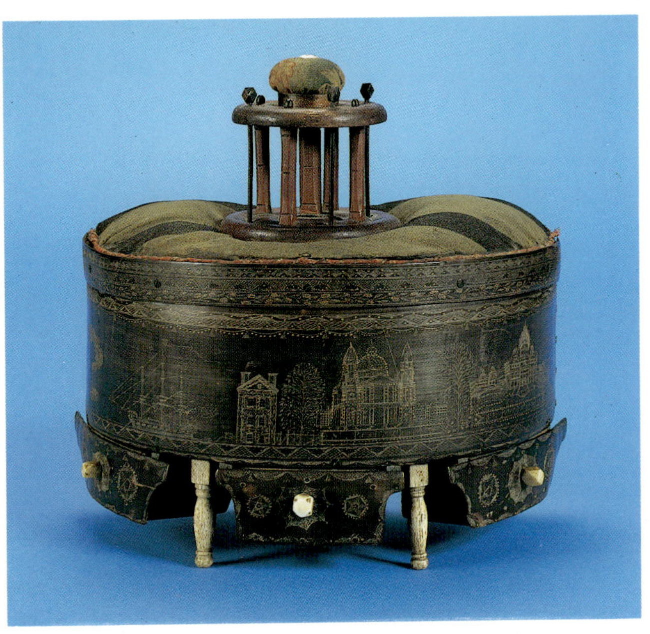

Sewing Box

*1840-60, Unknown Artist, probably United States,
10 x 10 x 5 inches, incised baleen, carved ivory, carved, sawed,
and turned wood, lined and cotton fabrics, and paint, Private Collection.*

Seamen often used spare moments on long voyages to whittle and carve tokens for their loved ones. While this sewing box was probably not the work of a professional woodworker, the skillful incorporation of baleen, ivory, wood, and nautical imagery suggests that it was the creation of a clever craftsman aboard a whaling vessel.

The box is simply constructed. The demi-lune shape is fronted with a wide strip of baleen. The bottom is painted blue. Centered on the padded linen top is a whittled spool holder with diamond-headed pins. The box surmounts three baleen-faced hanging drawers. Each has an ivory pull which matches the heads of the spool holder pins. The entire box perches on four carved ivory legs.

Great care is lavished on the designs incised on the baleen. A variety of patterns borders the main composition. The main images call to mind a lengthy voyage and read from left to right: a lighthouse, a ship with two stacks, and a three-masted sailing ship. The far shore is indicated by a tall house and tree, which are followed by clearly labeled representations of St. Paul's and St. Peter's cathedrals. At the extreme right edge, a large flag flutters from a mast, while the image of a whale underscores the nature of the long journey. OCT

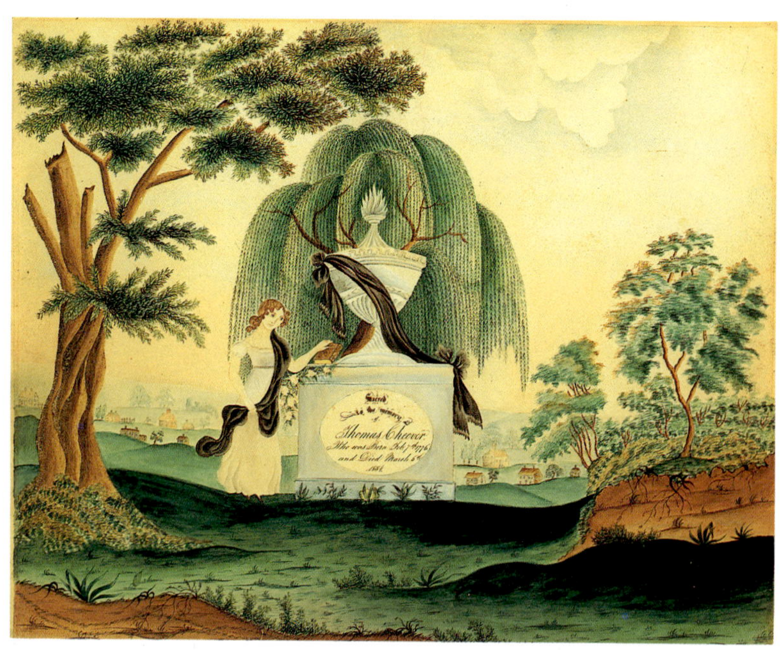

Mourning Picture for Thomas Cheever

Ca. 1821, attributed to Sally F. Cheever, 1806-1831, Danvers, Massachusetts, $18\frac{5}{16}$ x $22\frac{1}{4}$ inches, watercolor with pen and brown ink on paper, Collection of Dr. James and Susan Widder.

In the early nineteenth century, the death rate among families, especially children, was extremely high. To honor the memory of the deceased, mourning pictures were created and hung in the parlors of many homes.

The first mourning pictures were embroidered in silk by young schoolgirls. Watercolor was often added and, as in this picture attributed to Sally F. Cheever, paper eventually replaced the expensive linen.

In keeping with the tradition, Cheever has carefully painted specific areas, such as the leaves of the trees, to simulate the complex stitching of needlework. The standard neoclassical elements of mourning have also been included: a grieving relative, a tomb adorned with an urn, a weeping willow tree and a small row of houses in a landscape setting.

Sally F. Cheever is thought to have made a number of mourning pictures for other members of her family as well, including two sisters who died in infancy. This picture for Thomas Cheever was painted in advance with the inscription added by another hand. DK

Birdhouse

1920s (poss.), Unknown Artist, southern United States, 19½ x 9½ x 11½ inches, carved and painted wood, and wire, Collection of Lois and Richard Rosenthal.

While carved wooden objects have become the most widely collected form of folk art, very little of it can be identified as coming from the South. This piece can trace its origin of purchase to North Carolina. As a birdhouse it is a rare carved form among others such as decoys, whirligigs, shop signs and decorative carvings.

This example was originally painted in natural colors with the yellow hat suggesting a straw boater. Such straw hats were especially common in the hot climate of the South. The Birdhouse was meant to hang by the wire from the branch of a tree. The base was probably added later. Birds found protection nesting in the hollow of the mouth, just as in the hollow of a tree. The opening suggests it was meant for a large bird, such as a robin. The sensitive, whimsical quality of the head combines with utility to wed form and function in a very complementary, delightful manner. AJE

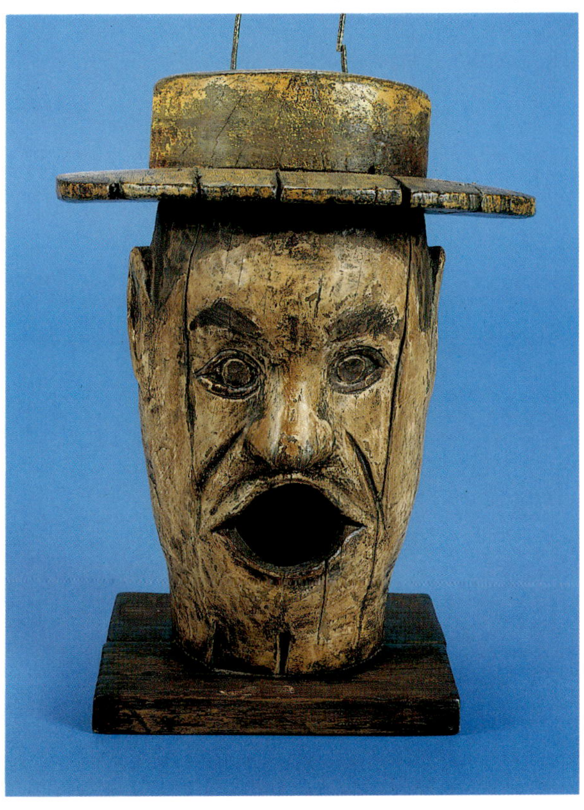

Cigar Store Indian

*Ca. 1870s, Julius Theodore Melchers, 1829-1909, Detroit, Michigan,
80½ x 18 x 15½ inches, carved and painted wood,
signed on medal with a carved and painted script "M,"
Collection of Mr. and Mrs. William Gilmore.*

During his lifetime Julius Melchers was perhaps the best-known carver of Cigar Store Indians. An immigrant from Prussia, he advertised for over thirty-six years in Detroit directories as "Sculptor, Modeler and Wood Carver." He had one of the largest and best collections of Native American artifacts in the state of Michigan, and reportedly authentically costumed his Cigar Store Indians.

Carved in one piece from an old ship's mast, this example is possibly a portrait of Chief Black Hawk of the Sauk and Fox people originally from the Great Lakes area of Wisconsin. Melchers owned a buckskin hunting shirt which belonged to Black Hawk, and carved the Chief more than once.

Melcher's Indians, whether portraits or ideal figures, display a simple, straightforward pose with an air of elegance and dignity. This one is signed by the artist with a script M on the medal hanging from the Indian's neck. Melchers used this as a signature. It is a rare example of a signed piece. AJE

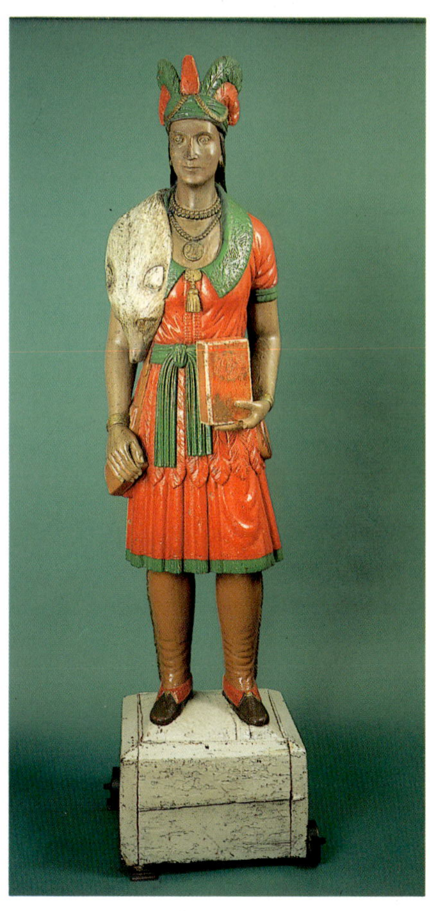

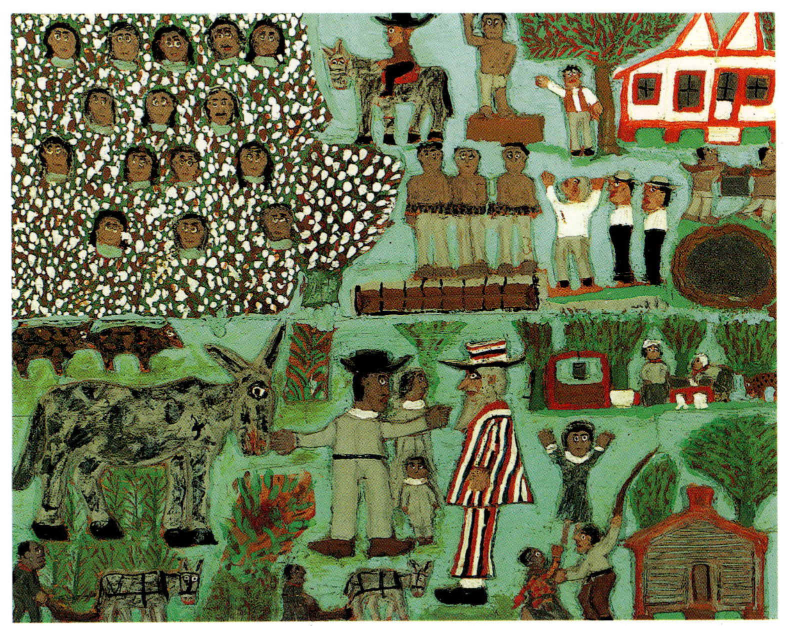

Slave Time

1965-70, Elijah Pierce, 1892-1984, Columbus, Ohio, 28½ x 35 inches, carved and painted wood, Collection of Alice and Richard Guggenheim.

An African-American barber in Columbus, Ohio, Elijah Pierce heard tales of slavery from his father and depicted them in his wood carvings. This relief is the first by Elijah Pierce on the subject of slavery. It was purchased from the artist at his barber shop in 1972.

In the upper left corner slaves working in a cotton field are being supervised by an overseer on his horse. In the upper center a slave is being auctioned next to the overseer's house with three white-shirted spectators below. To the right of the spectators is a pond with two slaves carrying food above. To the left of the spectators are three slaves in chains eating from a trough.

In the lower half to the right are scenes of slaves washing clothes, a slave being whipped, and a slave cabin. In the lower half to the left is a scene after the Emancipation. A freed slave is demanding his forty acres and a mule from Uncle Sam. Below this, freed slaves are working the land. AJE

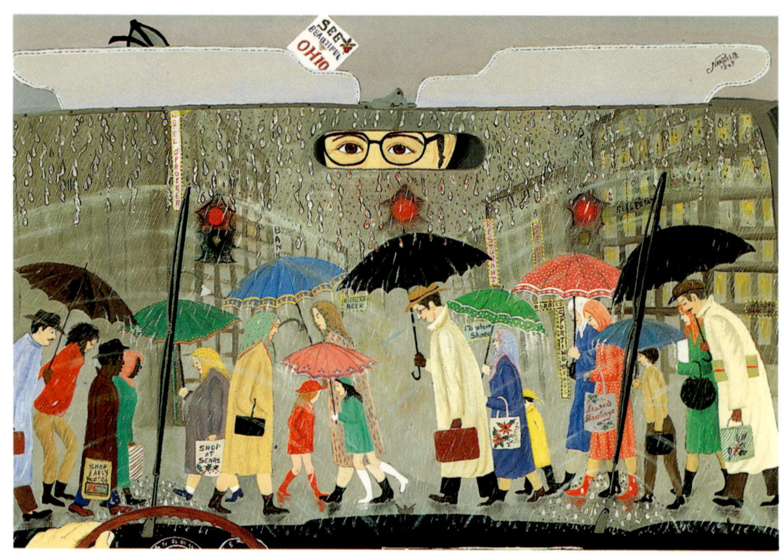

The Eyes of a Truck Driver

1969, Nan Phelps, b. 1904, Hamilton, Ohio, $34\frac{1}{4}$ x 24 inches, signed and dated, upper right, "Nan Phelps 1969," oil on canvasboard, Collection of Lois and Richard Rosenthal.

Nan Phelps, the daughter of a country minister, was born in London, Kentucky, in 1904. In 1922 she married and moved to Hamilton, Ohio, where she raised her five children. In addition to family responsibilities, Phelps managed to take occasional art classes at the Art Academy of Cincinnati. Her work was exhibited at the Cincinnati Art Museum in the 1930s and 1940s, and two paintings are included in the Museum's permanent collection. In recent years Nan's paintings have received national attention through exhibitions and stories in art journals.

The life experiences that Nan, as we have come to know her, records are effervescent. Her recollections of growing up in Kentucky are vividly described in hundreds of works made over the decades. In this painting, *The Eyes of a Truck Driver,* she investigates the world through another's frame of reference, a truck driver. Seen from inside the truck, windshield wipers flap against the pelting rain as colorfully clad Christmas shoppers hurry across the street. The dismal day is undaunting; the artist tucks a brochure, "See Beautiful Ohio," inside the interior visor. GG

Table and Tray

1940s, Anna Bernardine Kessler, 1911-1989, Lancaster, Ohio, table 26½ x 25 x 15¼ inches, tray 10½ x 13¼ x 1 inches, pieced and painted wood, and painted tin, Private Collection.

Anna Bernardine Kessler lived at 159 E. Wheeling Street in Lancaster, Ohio, with her father, mother and sister. This artist, of German Catholic heritage, was never married or employed. After the death of her parents, followed by that of her sister in the early 1980s, Kessler moved to Christ's Nursing Home. At that time the house and its contents, including the table and tray, were sold.

Kessler used to visit her neighbor Mr. Delancy for free scrap wood. Mr. Delancy owned a lumber company. She pieced the scraps together to form furniture and then painted her creations. Sometimes she painted tin trays. She usually gave the furniture and trays away.

Kessler remembered making this table in her thirties. It was placed between the living room and the dining room where it held the telephone. The tray was made to match it. The repeated tulip decoration is elegant and masterful in its simplicity, and the overall color scheme wonderfully unifies the form. AJE

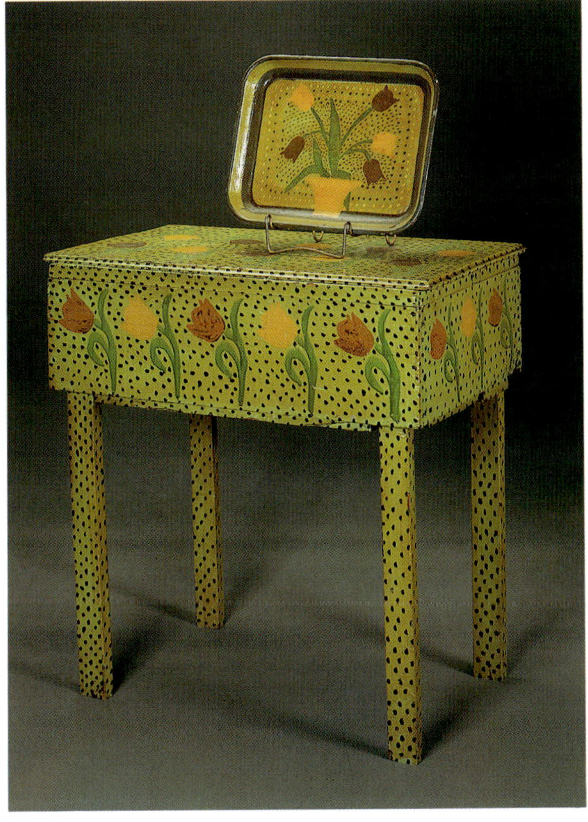

Three Pigs

Early 20th century, Unknown Artist, 18 x 22 inches, oil on canvas, Collection of Alice and Richard Guggenheim.

As the inscription across the bottom of the canvas proudly proclaims, these three pigs are the prized possessions of Samuel Crampton of Colett, Indiana. Animal "portraits" of award-winning livestock are part of a long agrarian tradition that became popular in the mid-eighteenth century. Itinerant painters were commissioned to record the images of breeds with particularly outstanding or peculiar qualities. As in this case, the artist has captured the singular desirability of these animals, their fatness. Here group portraiture is the *mise-en-scene*. As is customary, the animals are symmetrically arranged and presented in profile. The diminution of spatial recession is ignored in order to present the animals equally sized. Special emphasis is given to the shadows cast by the pigs, as well as the broad landscape, signifying a land-rich owner. GG

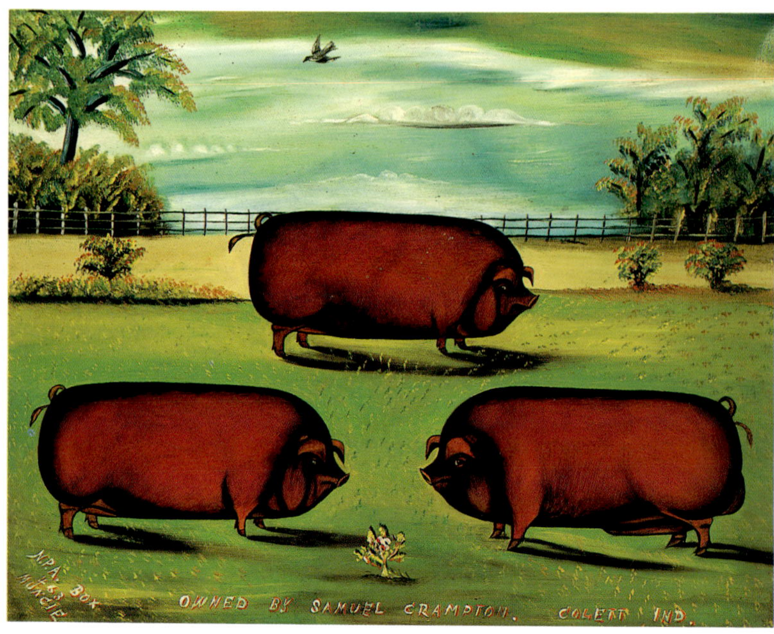

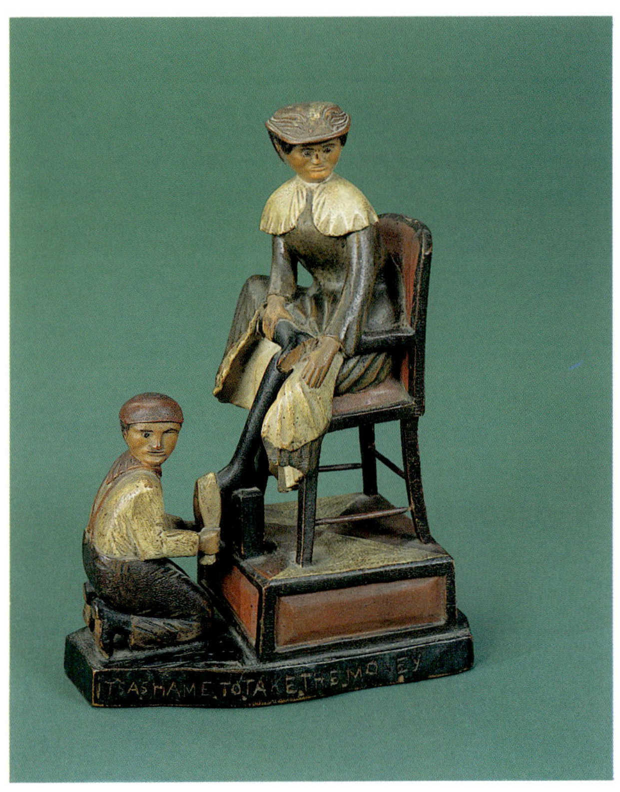

It's a Shame to Take the Money

Ca. 1900-10, Unknown Artist, Kentucky, 10 x 7¼ x 4⅜ inches, painted and carved wood with glass eyes in the woman, Collection of Mr. and Mrs. Tom Porter.

This piece came from Kentucky with two other sculptural groups by the same hand. This example is undated; the others were dated 1902 and 1908. None of the three were signed. Here there is a slightly risqué anecdote. The shoe shine boy finds that he can peek into the dress of the woman. Winking and looking at the viewer, he quips, ''It's a shame to take the money.''

The motif used by the sculptor is strikingly similar to a calendar illustration of the same period advertising ''Toney's Shoe Shining Parlor.'' The paint is probably original. The boy's remark is incised along the base. Wonderfully witty, this sculpture reveals human emotions of everyday life. As such, it is a didactic statement about the time, its humor and culture. AJE

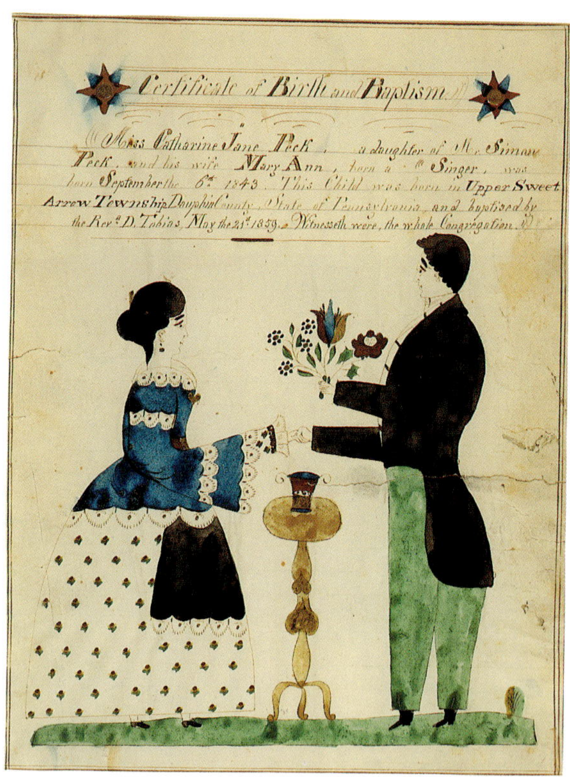

Fractur – Certificate of Birth and Baptism for Catharine Jane Peck

1859, Henry Young, 1792-1861, Centre County, Pennsylvania, 11¾ x 7⅞ inches, pen and brown ink, watercolor on lined wove paper, Collection of Cincinnati Art Museum, Gift of Dr. and Mrs. J. Louis Ransohoff in memory of Carol R. Guggenheim, 1958.341.

As a parochial schoolteacher in Union County, Pennsylvania, Henry Young, like many of his colleagues, supplemented his meager income by making fracturs, colorful certificates of birth, baptism, marriage and death. The term "fractur" was initially derived from a sixteenth-century style of lettering or calligraphy. Today, however, it often refers to both the script and painted decoration found in many of the Pennsylvania German manuscripts.

Henry Young created over a dozen basic formats for his fractur designs. This example showing a man and woman with flowers and small feet was one of his most popular. The two eight-pointed stars above the text, the curious yellow and green bush, the tiny flowers in the woman's dress and the double lines in the margin are characteristic motifs found in this particular format.

As Young got older and demand for his fracturs increased, he prepared his designs in advance and filled in the blanks with each commission. Like this certificate, his later works are less detailed, but still very colorful and carefully crafted. DK

Morey Machine Shop

1955, Ralph Fasanella, b. 1914, Hartsdale, New York, 60 x 48 inches, signed and dated, lower left, "R. Fasanella 1955," oil on canvas, Private Collection.

The *joie de vivre* associated with folk art is not a part of Ralph Fasanella's repertoire. Born in Greenwich Village in 1914 to the family of an ice delivery man, Fasanella made labor-union·activism his big business. As a CIO organizer, he marched for workers' rights with the enthusiasm of an evangelical preacher. In 1945 when he was labeled as a Communist and was repeatedly shut out of jobs, Fasanella turned to pumping gas and painting to survive. By glorifying the working class, his paintings parallel Social Realism of the nineteenth century.

Morey Machine Shop, one of Fasanella's finest works, depicts a shop where he worked as a bench hand in 1955. The shop was in Long Island City and manufactured lathes. In the painting everything is minutely described: machinery, Flo's Lunch Cart, a reception in the foreground, time cards hanging on the wall, the boss's office, even the rafters above. In spite of the banality of the scene, the painting is infused with Fasanella's wit; the lathe being pushed in the foreground is labeled "MONEY" rather than Morey, the name of the shop. According to the artist, "Morey's was a United Electrical Workers of America CIO shop and one of the better ones. It was one of the nine places the FBI knocked me out of." (Nicholas Pileggi, "Portrait of the Artist as a Garage Attendant in the Bronx," *New York*, October 30, 1972, p. 45.) GG

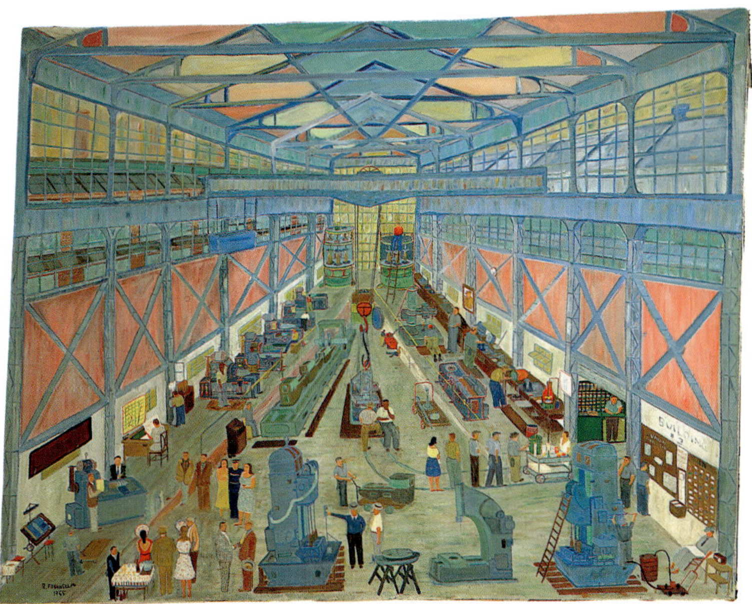

Pair of Hinges

18th century, Unknown Artist, Pennsylvania,
a) 11¼ x 38¼ x 3¾ inches, b) 11⅛ x 38 x 3¾ inches, wrought iron,
Collection of Dr. and Mrs. Kenneth Kreines.

The Pair of Hinges was purchased at the annual New Year's Day auction, 1989, at Litchfield Auction Gallery, Litchfield, Connecticut. They were formerly in the Harold Corbin Collection of American Iron that was exhibited at the Shelburne Museum in Vermont throughout the summer of 1988.

The door hinges are extremely well wrought with sword ends, scrolled decoration and ram's horn side ornaments. The size of the pieces adds to their mastery and gives them a sculptural appearance. The blacksmith wrought the iron at a red or white heat. There was little or no time for measuring except using his eye as a guide. Considering that the hinges were without doubt made with a particular door in mind, exactness of size and spontaneity in manufacture made great demands on the skill of the smith. The hinges are so large and so fine that they were probably made for a very important building. AJE

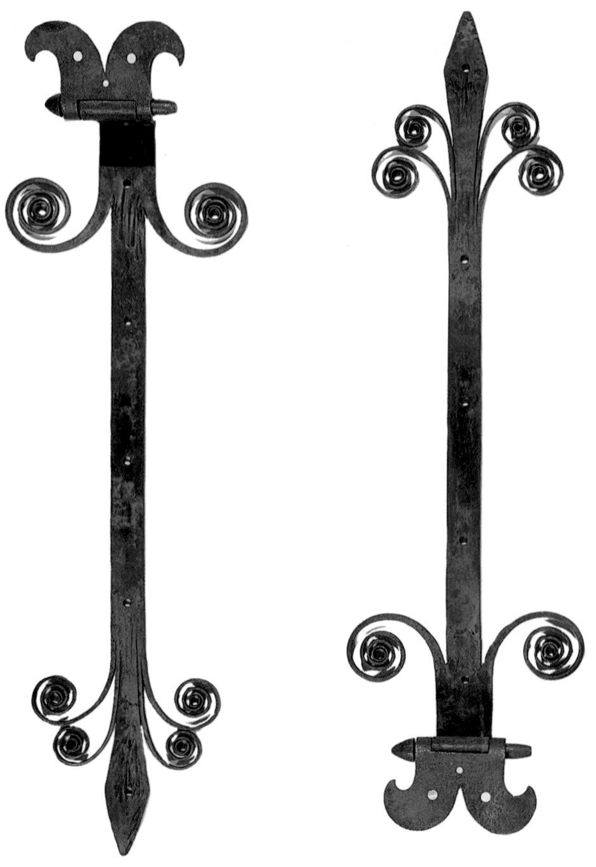